Collins

Cambridge Lower Secondary

Maths

PROGRESS BOOK 8: STUDENT'S BOOK

Author: Alastair Duncombe

William Collins' dream of knowledge for all began with the publication of his first book in 1819.
A self-educated mill worker, he not only enriched millions of lives, but also founded a flourishing publishing house.
Today, staying true to this spirit, Collins books are packed with inspiration, innovation and practical expertise.
They place you at the centre of a world of possibility and give you exactly what you need to explore it.

Collins. Freedom to teach.

Published by Collins

An imprint of HarperCollinsPublishers
The News Building, 1 London Bridge Street, London, SE1 9GF, UK

HarperCollinsPublishers
Macken House, 39/40 Mayor Street Upper, Dublin 1, D01 C9W8, Ireland

Browse the complete Collins catalogue at
collins.co.uk

British Library Cataloguing-in-Publication Data
A catalogue record for this publication is available from the British Library.

The questions and accompanying marks included in this resource have been written by the author and are for guidance only.
They do not replicate examination papers and the questions in this resource will not appear in your exams. In examinations
the way marks are awarded may be different. Any references to assessment and/or assessment preparation are the author's
interpretation of the syllabus requirements.

This text has not been through the endorsement process for the Cambridge Pathway. Any references or materials related
to answers, grades, papers or examinations are based on the opinion of the author. The Cambridge International Education
syllabus or curriculum framework associated assessment guidance material and specimen papers should always be referred to
for definitive guidance.

Author: Alastair Duncombe
Publisher: Elaine Higgleton
Product manager: Catherine Martin
Product developer: Saaleh Patel
Copyeditor: Eric Pradel
Proofreader: Tim Jackson
Cover designer: Gordon MacGilp
Cover illustrator: Ann Paganuzzi
Typesetter: Ken Vail Graphic Design
Production controller: Sarah Hovell
Printed in India by Multivista Global Pvt. Ltd.

MIX
Paper | Supporting
responsible forestry
FSC™ C007454

This book is produced from independently certified FSC™ paper to ensure responsible forest management.
For more information visit: www.harpercollins.co.uk/green

Content

Introduction

This *Stage 8 Progress Student's Book* supports the *Collins Cambridge Stage 8 Lower Secondary Maths course*.

This book contains
- six Assessment Tasks – each corresponding to 4 or 5 chapters in the Collins Cambridge Stage 8 Maths course
- two End of Book Tests – Paper 1 is a non-calculator paper and Paper 2 is a calculator-allowed paper
- Self-assessment sheets for each of the Assessment Tasks and End of Book Tests

How to use the Progress resources

This Student's Book contains a range of Assessment Tasks and Tests that are designed to assess your learning. They can be used to identify your strengths and weaknesses. The resources can also be used by your teachers to guide their teaching to make sure you make the best possible progress through the course.

The six Assessment Tasks could be used as class tests or your teachers may ask you to complete them at home. Each Task includes a list of the topics being tested, and begins with some multiple-choice questions. These starting questions are designed to help build confidence and to check your understanding of some key ideas. As you work through each task, you will find the questions become more challenging. You will find that some questions are designed to be answered without a calculator, whilst a calculator is allowed in other questions.

Some of the questions in each Task are written to address the Cambridge *Thinking and Working Mathematically* characteristics:
- Specialising and generalising
- Conjecturing and convincing
- Characterising and classifying
- Critiquing and improving.

These questions may require you to think more deeply. You may also need to explain your answer or show clear working out.

The End of Book tests contain questions assessing the topics you will have covered in the whole year. The style of the End of Book tests is the same as the Assessment Tasks, with a mixture of question styles and question difficulties, as well as the inclusion of some Thinking and Working Mathematically questions. Your teachers may use these tests to assess your progress during the year.

The Self-assessment sheets give you the opportunity to reflect on your understanding. You record the mark for each question in the grids and then use these to find how well you have done with the questions relating to each chapter (or, for the End of Book Tests, each mathematics strand). This allows you to then reflect on which parts of the test went well and which areas you found harder. You could pick out particular chapters as strengths or weaknesses. You could also comment on your success with *Thinking and Working Mathematically* questions or how you did on calculator or non-calculator questions.

The Self-assessment sheets also prompt you to set some targets. Try not to set targets that are too general. You are more likely to achieve your targets if you write something more specific. For example,

Less helpful targets…

To become more confident at decimals ✗

To avoid making needless errors ✗

More helpful targets…

To become more confident at dividing a decimal by a whole number ✓

To try to avoid making needless errors by underlining key words in the question ✓

Key features: Assessment Tasks

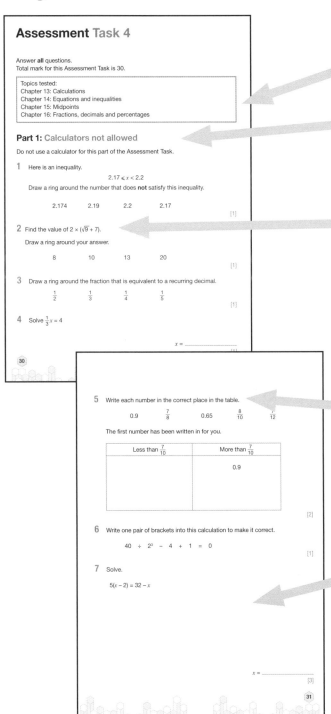

Assessment Task 4

Answer **all** questions.
Total mark for this Assessment Task is 30.

Topics tested:
Chapter 13: Calculations
Chapter 14: Equations and inequalities
Chapter 15: Midpoints
Chapter 16: Fractions, decimals and percentages

Part 1: Calculators not allowed

Do not use a calculator for this part of the Assessment Task.

1 Here is an inequality.

$$2.17 \leqslant x < 2.2$$

Draw a ring around the number that does **not** satisfy this inequality.

2.174   2.19   2.2   2.17

[1]

2 Find the value of $2 \times (\sqrt{9} + 7)$.

Draw a ring around your answer.

8   10   13   20

[1]

3 Draw a ring around the fraction that is equivalent to a recurring decimal.

$\frac{1}{2}$ $\frac{1}{3}$ $\frac{1}{4}$ $\frac{1}{5}$

[1]

4 Solve $\frac{1}{3}x = 4$

$x =$ _____

30

5 Write each number in the correct place in the table.

0.9 $\frac{7}{8}$ 0.65 $\frac{8}{10}$ $\frac{7}{12}$

The first number has been written in for you.

Less than $\frac{7}{10}$	More than $\frac{7}{10}$
	0.9

[2]

6 Write one pair of brackets into this calculation to make it correct.

$$40 \div 2^3 - 4 + 1 = 0$$

[1]

7 Solve.

$$5(x - 2) = 32 - x$$

$x =$ _____

[3]

31

At the top of each Assessment Task, you will find a list of the topics being covered.

You will be told whether you can use a calculator or not.

Each Task begins with some multiple-choice questions to boost your confidence and to assess key ideas.

Each Task contains some questions that relate to Thinking and Working Mathematically. You may have to think more deeply in these questions.

Each question is worded clearly and there is plenty of space for you to show your working out.

Key features: Student self-assessment sheets

Assessment Task 1: Self-assessment

Enter the mark for each question in the unshaded cells below.

Question	Negative numbers, indices and roots	2D and 3D shapes	Collecting data	Factors and rational numbers
1				
2				
3				
4				
5				
6				
7				
8				
9				
10				
11				
12				
13				
14				
15				
16				
17				
18				
19				
20				
Total	/10	/9	/4	/7

Some of the questions test your skills at Thinking and Working Mathematically. Write your marks for these questions in the grid below.

Question number	6	7	8	14	16(b)	17	18	20	Total
Thinking and working mathematically									/13

The areas of the test that I am pleased with are

_____

_____

_____

The areas of the test that I found harder are

_____

_____

_____

Set yourself TWO targets.

TARGET 1

_____

TARGET 2

_____

Record the mark you scored in each question in the table.

Add up the marks in each column. The totals will help you to compare how you have done in each topic area.

There is space for you to reflect on how you have done and to set some targets.

Assessment Task 1

Answer **all** questions.
Total mark for this Assessment Task is 30.

> Topics tested:
> Chapter 1: Negative numbers, indices and roots
> Chapter 2: 2D and 3D shapes
> Chapter 3: Collecting data
> Chapter 4: Factors and rational numbers

Part 1: Calculators not allowed

Do not use a calculator for this part of the Assessment Task.

1   Draw a ring around the value of (–2) × (–5)

       –10   –7   7   10

[1]

2   Draw a ring around the value of 3^0

       0   1   3   30

[1]

3   Draw a ring around the cube root of –27

       –3   3   –9   9

[1]

4   Find the prime factorisation of 60

_____

[2]

5 Calculate.

20 ÷ (–5)

_____

(–36) ÷ (–4)

_____

[2]

6 Fatima draws a shape without any right angles.
Her shape is a type of kite.
In Fatima's shape, opposite angles are equal.

Write down the name of Fatima's shape.

_____

[1]

7 Pria and Aarush each think of a number.

| Pria's number is the square of –4 | | Aarush's number is less than 0 and is a square root of 36 |

Pria and Aarush add their numbers together to get a total.

Find the total of their numbers.

_____

[2]

8 Yana wants to find out what people in her town think about the railway station. She decides to collect her data either by doing interviews face-to-face or by giving out questionnaires.

(a) Write down one reason why she may want to collect her data by doing interviews face-to-face.

_____

_____

[1]

(b) Write down one reason why she may want to collect her data by giving out questionnaires.

_____

_____

[1]

9 The prime factorisation of 48 is $2^4 \times 3$
The lowest common multiple of 48 and a number y is $2^4 \times 3^2 \times 5$

Find the smallest possible value of y.

_____

[1]

10 Write 32^4 as a power of 2

_____

[2]

Part 2: Calculators allowed

You may use a calculator for this part of the Assessment Task.

11 A regular polygon has 16 lines of symmetry.

Draw a ring around the order of rotation symmetry for the polygon.

4	8	16	32

[1]

12 The radius of a circle is 9 cm.

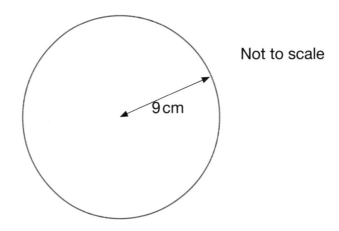

Not to scale

9 cm

Draw a ring around the calculation that gives the circumference of the circle in centimetres.

$$\frac{9}{\pi} \qquad \frac{18}{\pi} \qquad \pi \times 9 \qquad \pi \times 18$$

[1]

13 A factory has 100 workers that work full time and 50 workers that work part time.

Dave wants to select a sample of workers to complete a questionnaire. He wants the sample to be representative of the workers in the factory. Dave selects 10 full time workers.

Draw a ring around the number of part time workers he should select.

5	10	20	50

[1]

14 Tick (✓) to show if each statement is true or false.

	True	False
All rectangles are squares.	☐	☐
All squares are parallelograms.	☐	☐
All parallelograms are trapeziums.	☐	☐

[1]

15 The prime factorisation of 220 is $2^2 \times 5 \times 11$
The prime factorisation of 264 is $2^3 \times 3 \times 11$

Find the highest common factor of 220 and 264

_____

[2]

16 Euler's formula is $V + F - E = 2$

(a) A polyhedron has 9 faces and 16 edges.

Work out the number of vertices for this polyhedron.

_____

[1]

(b) Sophia has a polyhedron.

She says, "My polyhedron has 8 edges, 6 vertices and 12 faces."

Tick (✓) to show if Sophia could be correct or not.

She could be correct ☐   She is not correct ☐

Use Euler's formula to explain your answer.

_____

_____

_____

[1]

5

17 The Venn diagram shows the hierarchy of natural numbers, integers and rational numbers.

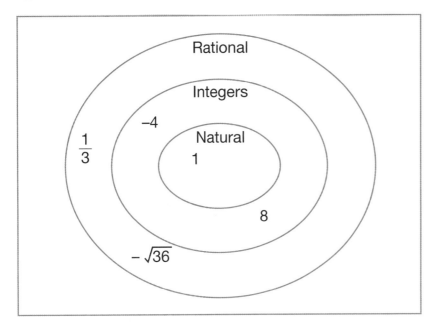

Draw a ring around each number that has not been put into the Venn diagram correctly.

$$\frac{1}{3} \qquad -\sqrt{36} \qquad -4 \qquad 1 \qquad 8$$

[2]

18 Aki wants to collect a sample of 20 people from his school.
He samples the first 20 people he sees one lunchtime.

Explain why Aki may not get reliable data.

_____

_____

_____

[1]

19 Here is a mathematical statement.

$$5^n \div 5^3 = 5^4$$

Find the value of n.

$n =$ _____

[1]

20 The diagram shows a circle and a square.

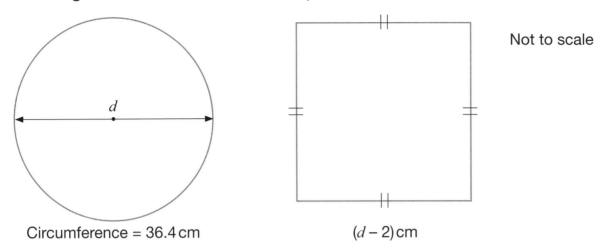

Not to scale

Circumference = 36.4 cm

$(d - 2)$ cm

The circle has circumference 36.4 cm.
The side length of the square is 2 cm less than the diameter of the circle.

Show that the perimeter of the square is greater than the circumference of the circle.

[3]

Total marks: $\dfrac{}{30}$

Assessment Task 1: Self-assessment

Enter the mark for each question in the unshaded cells below.

Question	Negative numbers, indices and roots	2D and 3D shapes	Collecting data	Factors and rational numbers
1				
2				
3				
4				
5				
6				
7				
8				
9				
10				
11				
12				
13				
14				
15				
16				
17				
18				
19				
20				
Total	/10	/9	/4	/7

Some of the questions test your skills at Thinking and Working Mathematically. Write your marks for these questions in the grid below.

Question number	6	7	8	14	16(b)	17	18	20	Total
Thinking and working mathematically									/13

The areas of the test that I am pleased with are

_____

_____

_____

The areas of the test that I found harder are

_____

_____

_____

Set yourself TWO targets.

TARGET 1

_____

_____

TARGET 2

_____

_____

Assessment Task 2

Answer **all** questions.
Total mark for this Assessment Task is 30.
You will need mathematical instruments.

> Topics tested:
> Chapter 5: Expressions
> Chapter 6: Angles
> Chapter 7: Place value, rounding and decimals
> Chapter 8: Presenting and interpreting data 1

Part 1: Calculators not allowed

Do not use a calculator for this part of the Assessment Task.

1 Draw a ring around the value of $4a + 15$ when $a = -2$

7	17	23	52

[1]

2 Draw a ring around the bearing that is the same as the direction West.

090°	180°	270°	300°

[1]

3 Find the value of $5 \div 0.5$

Draw a ring around your answer.

0.1	1	2.5	10

[1]

4 Draw connecting lines to match each expression on the left with an expression without brackets on the right.

$6(n + 2)$	$8n + 32$
$8(n + 4)$	$6n + 32$
$2(3n + 16)$	$6n + 12$
$4(2n + 3)$	$8n + 12$

[1]

5 Here are the heights (in metres) of 12 apple trees.

| 9.4 | 8.7 | 7.7 | 7.4 | 8.1 | 7.2 |
| 6.8 | 8.7 | 9.1 | 7.6 | 7.2 | 7.5 |

(a) Complete all the columns in the frequency table to record these heights.

All class intervals in the first column should have the same width.

Height, x (metres)	Tally	Frequency
$6 \leqslant x < 7$		
$7 \leqslant x < 8$		
___ $\leqslant x <$ ___		
___ $\leqslant x <$ ___		

[3]

(b) Ben draws this stem-and-leaf diagram to show the heights of the trees.

```
6 | 8
7 | 7  4  2  6  2
8 | 7  1  7
9 | 4  1
```

Key: 6 | 8 represents a height of 6.8 metres

Write down **two** mistakes Ben has made in his stem-and-leaf diagram.

Mistake 1 _____

_____

Mistake 2 _____

_____

[2]

6 Round 0.040693 to 3 significant figures.

_____

[1]

7 Write these calculations in order of size, starting with the calculation that gives the smallest answer.

154×0.01 $0.11 \div 0.01$ $0.31 \div 0.1$

_____   _____   _____

        smallest   largest

[1]

8 Work out the size of the angle marked x.

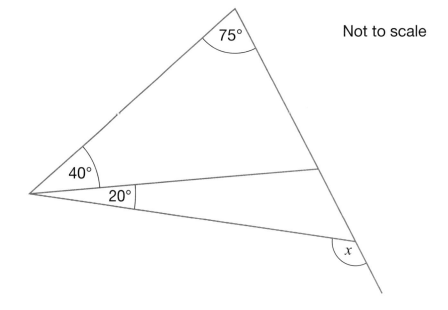

75°

Not to scale

40°

20°

x

_____ °

[2]

9 Work out the value of 0.46×0.86

_____

[2]

12

Part 2: Calculators allowed

You may use a calculator for this part of the Assessment Task.

10 Round 16 465 to 2 significant figures.
Draw a ring around your answer.

16   17   16 000   17 000

[1]

11 The stem-and-leaf diagram shows the lengths of some animals.

```
11 | 5
12 | 1   4   9
13 | 0   2   7   8   8
14 | 3   5   5   6   7   9
15 | 9
```

Key: 11 | 5   represents   11.5 cm

Draw a ring around the length of the longest animal.

9 cm   1.59 cm   15.9 cm   159 cm

[1]

12 Draw a ring around the formula.

7          $4n + 5 = 29$ $2(3p - 1)$ $C = \pi D$

[1]

13 Here is an expression: $2x^2 + 3$
Nancy and Ravi both try to work out the value of the expression when $x = -4$

Nancy's work	Ravi's work
$x^2 = -16$	$2x = -8$
$2x^2 = -32$	$2x^2 = 64$
$2x^2 + 3 = -29$	$2x^2 + 3 = 67$

Tick (✓) to show if each student's work is correct or not.

	Correct	Not correct
Nancy's work		
Ravi's work	☐	☐

[1]

14 *AB* and *CD* are parallel lines.

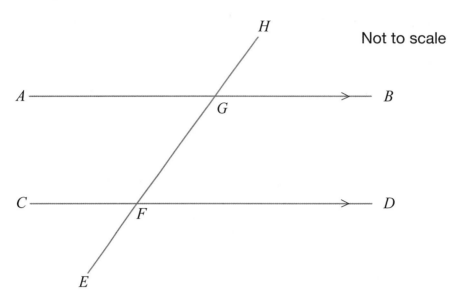

Not to scale

Here are four angles.

| Angle *CFG*   Angle *CFE*   Angle *HGB*   Angle *AGF* |

Write one of the angles from the box to complete each statement correctly.

Angle _____ is a corresponding angle to angle *GFD*.

Angle _____ is an alternate angle to angle *GFD*.

Angle _____ is vertically opposite angle *GFD*.

[2]

15 Factorise.

$12a^3b + 30a^2b^2$

_____

[2]

16 A sports team wants to change the colour of its shirt to either blue or yellow.
The team asks three groups of people which colour they prefer.
The incomplete table and the compound bar chart show some information
about the preferences of the three groups.

	Group 1	Group 2	Group 3
Blue		14	32
Yellow	24		20

(a) Complete the compound bar chart.

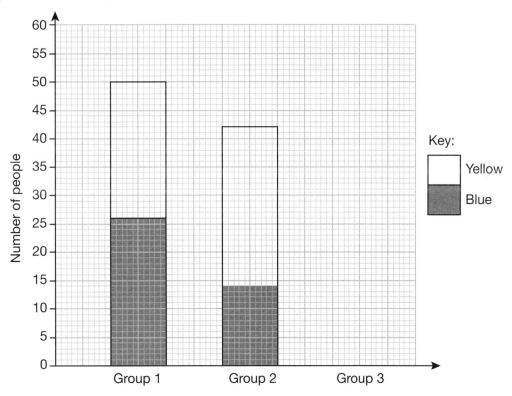

[2]

(b) Calculate the total number of people in the groups who prefer the
colour yellow.

_____

[1]

(c) Compare the shirt colour preferences of the people in Group 1 with the
preferences of people in Group 2.

_____

_____

[1]

15

17 The diagram shows the position of a swimming pool S and a cinema C.

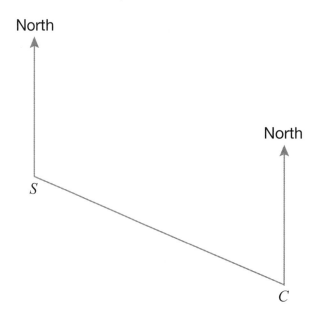

Measure the bearing of the swimming pool from the cinema.

_____ °

[1]

18 Alexa has m books.
Carlos has 4 **less** books than Alexa.
Lily has twice as many books as Carlos.
Somchai has 10 more books than Lily.

Find an expression for the number of books Somchai has.
Give your answer in terms of m and in its simplest form.

_____

[2]

Total marks: ——— 30

Assessment Task 2: Self-assessment

Enter the mark for each question in the unshaded cells below.

Question	Expressions	Angles	Place value, rounding and decimals	Presenting and interpreting data 1
1				
2				
3				
4				
5				
6				
7				
8				
9				
10				
11				
12				
13				
14				
15				
16				
17				
18				
Total	/8	/6	/6	/10

Some of the questions test your skills at Thinking and Working Mathematically. Write your marks for these questions in the grid below.

Question number	4	5(b)	13	14	Total
Thinking and working mathematically					/6

The areas of the test that I am pleased with are

_____

_____

_____

The areas of the test that I found harder are

_____

_____

_____

Set yourself TWO targets.

TARGET 1

_____

_____

TARGET 2

_____

_____

Assessment Task 3

Answer **all** questions.
Total mark for this Assessment Task is 30.

> Topics tested:
> Chapter 9: Functions and formulae
> Chapter 10: Fractions
> Chapter 11: Length, area and volume
> Chapter 12: Probability 1

Part 1: Calculators not allowed

Do not use a calculator for this part of the Assessment Task.

1 Here is a function machine.

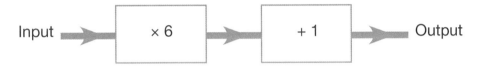

Draw a ring around the output when the input is 4

$$0.5 \qquad 11 \qquad 25 \qquad 30$$

[1]

2 Draw a ring around the value of $6 - 1\frac{3}{5}$

$$5\frac{3}{5} \qquad 5\frac{2}{5} \qquad 4\frac{3}{5} \qquad 4\frac{2}{5}$$

[1]

3 Draw a ring around the number of kilometres that 1 mile is approximately equal to.

$$0.16 \qquad 0.6 \qquad 1 \qquad 1.6$$

[1]

4 The probability that Seema buys bananas when she goes to the supermarket is 0.85

Find the probability that she does **not** buy bananas when she goes to the supermarket.

_____

[1]

5 Find the area of the parallelogram.

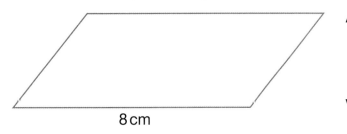

Not to scale

4 cm

8 cm

_____ cm²

[1]

6 Toby sells cakes to customers and delivers them by post.
Each cake costs $2
He charges a fixed postage cost of $5 for each order.

Find a formula for the total cost, $C, for an order of n cakes.

$C =$ _____

[1]

7 Calculate $15 \div \frac{5}{6}$

_____

[2]

8 Lucy has a sequence of calculations.

Calculation 1 $2 \times 2\frac{1}{2} = 2 \times \frac{5}{2} = 5$

Calculation 2 $3 \times 2\frac{1}{3} = 3 \times \frac{7}{3} =$ _____

Calculation 3 $4 \times 2\frac{1}{4} =$ _____ $\times$ _____ $=$ _____

(a) Complete Lucy's work for calculations 2 and 3

[2]

(b) Lucy says,

     'One calculation in my sequence has an answer equal to 14'

     Give a reason why Lucy must be wrong.

_____

_____

[1]

9 Here are two trapeziums.

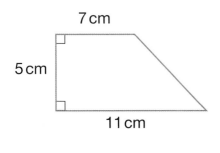

Trapezium A

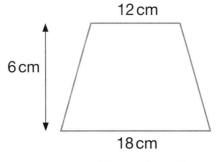

12 cm

Not to scale

6 cm

18 cm

Trapezium B

Tick (✓) to show if each statement is true or false.

	True	False
Area of trapezium A = 45 cm²	☐	☐
Area of trapezium B = 2 × (area of trapezium A)	☐	☐

[1]

10 Sanjay needs $4\frac{4}{5}$ kg of flour.

He has $2\frac{7}{8}$ kg of flour.

Calculate how much extra flour he needs.
Give your answer as a mixed number in its simplest form.

_____ kg

[3]

Part 2: Calculators allowed

You may use a calculator for this part of the Assessment Task.

11 Here is a formula.

$$A = \frac{n}{p}$$

Draw a ring around the correct rearrangement of this formula.

$$n = Ap \qquad n = A + p \qquad n = \frac{A}{p} \qquad n = A - p$$

[1]

12 Draw a ring around the surface area of the cuboid.

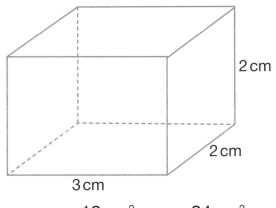

Not to scale

2 cm

2 cm

3 cm

$12 \, \text{cm}^2$ $\qquad$ $24 \, \text{cm}^2$ $\qquad$ $28 \, \text{cm}^2$ $\qquad$ $32 \, \text{cm}^2$

[1]

13 Here is a function machine.

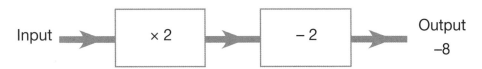

Input $\longrightarrow$ × 2 $\longrightarrow$ − 2 $\longrightarrow$ Output −8

The output is −8

Draw a ring around the value of the input.

$-2 \qquad\qquad -3 \qquad\qquad -18 \qquad\qquad -20$

[1]

14 Marta has a spinner with four sections.
The sections are numbered 1, 2, 3 and 4.
She spins her spinner 200 times.

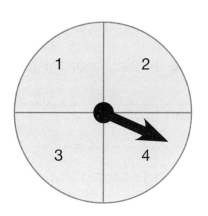

The table shows the results of her spins.

Number	1	2	3	4
Frequency	32	45	52	71

    (a) Find the relative frequency of the spinner landing on the
         section numbered 1

         _____

         [1]

    (b) Tick (✓) to show if you think Marta's spinner is likely to be fair or not.

         The spinner is likely to be fair ☐   The spinner is not likely to be fair ☐

         Explain your answer.
         You could use your answer to part **(a)** to help you.

         _____

         _____

         [1]

15 Here are some distances.

         35 miles   52 km   28 000 m

Write these distances in order of length, starting with the shortest.

    _____   _____   _____
      shortest   longest

         [1]

16 Here is a triangular prism.

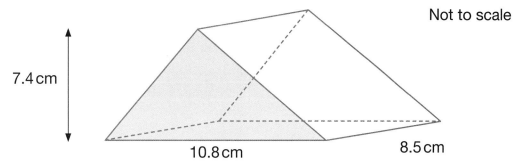

Not to scale

7.4 cm

10.8 cm

8.5 cm

The triangular cross-section has base 10.8 cm and perpendicular height 7.4 cm.
The length of the prism is 8.5 cm.

Find the volume of the prism.

_____ cm³

[2]

17 Here is a formula.

$$d = 3(p - a)$$

Make p the subject of the formula.

_____

[2]

18 The diagram shows the net of a square-based pyramid and a sketch of a cube.

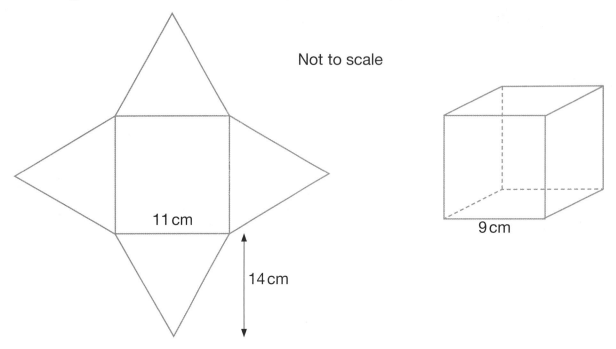

Not to scale

11 cm

14 cm

9 cm

All triangular faces of the pyramid are congruent.

Show that the surface area of the pyramid is less than the surface area of the cube.

[3]

19 The mapping diagram represents a function.

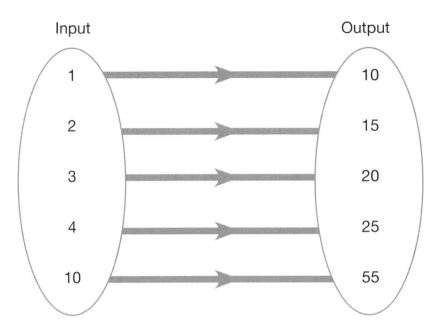

Input   Output

Find an expression for the output of the function if the input is x.
Give your answer in terms of x.

[2]

Total marks: $\dfrac{}{30}$

Assessment Task 3: Self-assessment

Enter the mark for each question in the unshaded cells below.

Question	Functions and formulae	Fractions	Length, area and volume	Probability 1
1				
2				
3				
4				
5				
6				
7				
8				
9				
10				
11				
12				
13				
14				
15				
16				
17				
18				
19				
Total	/8	/9	/10	/3

Some of the questions test your skills at Thinking and Working Mathematically. Write your marks for these questions in the grid below.

Question number	8(b)	9	14(b)	18	19	Total
Thinking and working mathematically						/8

The areas of the test that I am pleased with are

_____

_____

_____

The areas of the test that I found harder are

_____

_____

_____

Set yourself TWO targets.

TARGET 1

_____

_____

TARGET 2

_____

_____

Assessment Task 4

Answer **all** questions.
Total mark for this Assessment Task is 30.

> Topics tested:
> Chapter 13: Calculations
> Chapter 14: Equations and inequalities
> Chapter 15: Midpoints
> Chapter 16: Fractions, decimals and percentages

Part 1: Calculators not allowed

Do not use a calculator for this part of the Assessment Task.

1   Here is an inequality.

$$2.17 \leqslant x < 2.2$$

Draw a ring around the number that does **not** satisfy this inequality.

      2.174   2.19   2.2   2.17

[1]

2   Find the value of $2 \times (\sqrt{9} + 7)$.

Draw a ring around your answer.

      8   10   13   20

[1]

3   Draw a ring around the fraction that is equivalent to a recurring decimal.

      $\dfrac{1}{2}$ $\dfrac{1}{3}$ $\dfrac{1}{4}$ $\dfrac{1}{5}$

[1]

4   Solve $\dfrac{1}{3}x = 4$

$x = $ _____

[1]

5   Write each number in the correct place in the table.

$$0.9 \qquad \frac{7}{8} \qquad 0.65 \qquad \frac{8}{10} \qquad \frac{7}{12}$$

The first number has been written in for you.

Less than $\frac{7}{10}$	More than $\frac{7}{10}$
	0.9

[2]

6   Write one pair of brackets into this calculation to make it correct.

$$40 \ \div \ 2^3 \ - \ 4 \ + \ 1 \ = \ 0$$

[1]

7   Solve.

$$5(x - 2) = 32 - x$$

$x = $ _____

[3]

8 Write a decimal on each answer line to make correct statements.

    (a) $-5.4 <$ _____ < -5.32

                                                                                  [1]

    (b) $-\dfrac{11}{20} <$ _____ $\leqslant -\dfrac{1}{2}$

                                                                                  [1]

9 Calculate.

    (a) $100 \times 3.1 \times 0.04$

_____

                                                                                  [1]

    (b) $\dfrac{1}{4} \times 2\dfrac{3}{7} - \dfrac{1}{4} \times \dfrac{3}{7}$

_____

                                                                                   [2]

Part 2: Calculators allowed

You may use a calculator for this part of the Assessment Task.

10 Here is an inequality.

$$n \leqslant -1$$

Draw a ring around the largest possible integer value of n.

-2 -1 0 1

[1]

11 Draw a ring around the proportion that is greater than 60%.

8 out of 15   11 out of 24   16 out of 25   19 out of 32

[1]

12 Draw a ring around the midpoint of the line joining (3, 4) to (3, 10).

(0, 6)   (6, 14)   (3, 6)   (3, 7)

[1]

13 Tick (✓) the correct statements.

$\frac{7}{16} = 0.4375$ ☐

$\frac{8}{9}$ is equivalent to a recurring decimal   ☐

$\frac{11}{15}$ is equivalent to a terminating decimal   ☐

[1]

14 The inequality gives some information about a number t.

$$t \geqslant 6$$

Sam and Alicia make their own statements about t.

Sam's statement $\quad t + 1 > 7$

Alicia's statement $\quad 2t \geqslant 8$

Both statements contain an error.

Write correct versions of the statements by correcting the errors.

Sam's statement $\quad t + 1$ _____

Alicia's statement $\quad 2t$ _____

[1]

15 Here is some information about the number of students absent in two classes.

Class A	Class B
5 out of 32 students are absent.	3 out of 17 students are absent.

Tick (✓) the class that has the higher percentage of students absent.

Class A ☐ Class B ☐

Show how you worked out your answer.

[2]

16 The diagram shows a line segment AB.

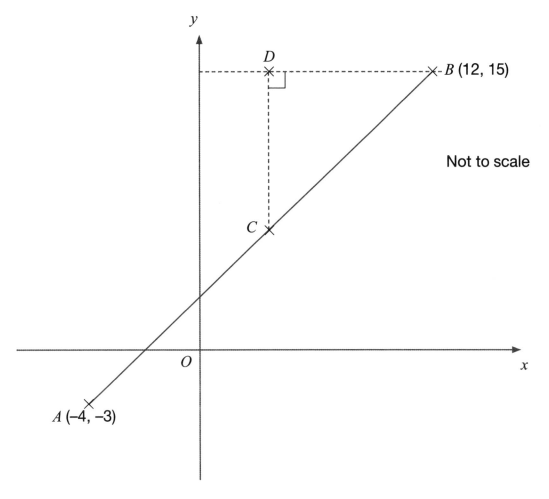

Not to scale

A is the point (–4, –3) and B is the point (12, 15).
C is the midpoint of AB.
D is the point vertically above C with angle $CDB = 90°$

(a) Find the coordinates of D.

(————, ————)

[2]

(b) E is a point vertically above D.

D is the midpoint of CE.

Find the coordinates of E.

(————, ————)

[1]

17 Complete these calculations by writing in the missing operations (+, −, × or ÷).
Each operation should be used exactly once.

$$(\sqrt{36} \underline{\quad} 2)^2 + 4 \underline{\quad} 5 = 36$$

$$(3^3 \underline{\quad} 13) \div (20 \underline{\quad} 4) = 8$$

[2]

18 Asim is n years old.
Heba says, 'To find my age, multiply Asim's age by 4 and subtract 11'
Layla says, 'To find my age, multiply Asim's age by 2 and then add 19'

Heba and Layla are the same age.

By forming and solving an equation, show that the total of the ages of Asim, Heba and Layla is more than 100 years.

[3]

Total marks: $\dfrac{\quad}{30}$

Assessment Task 4: Self-assessment

Enter the mark for each question in the unshaded cells below.

Question	Calculations	Equations and inequalities	Midpoints	Fractions, decimals and percentages
1				
2				
3				
4				
5				
6				
7				
8				
9				
10				
11				
12				
13				
14				
15				
16				
17				
18				
Total	/7	/10	/4	/9

Some of the questions test your skills at Thinking and Working Mathematically.
Write your marks for these questions in the grid below.

Question number	5	6	8	13	14	15	17	18	Total
Thinking and working mathematically									/14

The areas of the test that I am pleased with are

_____

_____

_____

The areas of the test that I found harder are

_____

_____

_____

Set yourself TWO targets.

TARGET 1

_____

_____

TARGET 2

_____

_____

Assessment Task 5

Answer **all** questions.
Total mark for this Assessment Task is 30.
You will need mathematical instruments.
Tracing paper may be used.

> Topics tested:
> Chapter 17: Presenting and interpreting data 2
> Chapter 18: Transformations
> Chapter 19: Percentages
> Chapter 20: Sequences

Part 1: Calculators not allowed

Do not use a calculator for this part of the Assessment Task.

1 A sequence is defined as

> First term is $2\frac{1}{2}$
>
> Term-to-term rule is: Add $1\frac{1}{2}$

Draw a ring around the 3rd term in the sequence.

$$4 \qquad\qquad 4\frac{1}{2} \qquad\qquad 5\frac{1}{2} \qquad\qquad 7$$

[1]

2 Draw a ring around the vector that corresponds to 7 units down.

$$\begin{pmatrix} 7 \\ 0 \end{pmatrix} \qquad \begin{pmatrix} -7 \\ 0 \end{pmatrix} \qquad \begin{pmatrix} 0 \\ 7 \end{pmatrix} \qquad \begin{pmatrix} 0 \\ -7 \end{pmatrix}$$

[1]

3 A coat costs \$400
The cost increases by 20%.

Draw a ring around the increase in cost of the coat.

$$\$20 \qquad\qquad \$40 \qquad\qquad \$80 \qquad\qquad \$100$$

[1]

4 Mike owns a bookshop.
He sells Fiction books, Non-fiction books and Biographies.
He draws this infographic to show the type of books he sold one day.

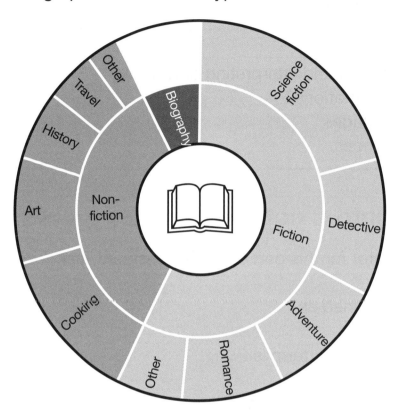

Tick (✓) to show if these statements are true or false.

	True	False
Mike sold more Non-fiction books than Biographies.	☐	☐
He sold more Romance books than Adventure books.	☐	☐
The type of Non-fiction book that sold most was Cooking.	☐	☐

[1]

5 A sequence has nth term rule $40 - 3n$

Find the 8th term in the sequence.

_____

[1]

6 A triangle T is drawn on the grid.

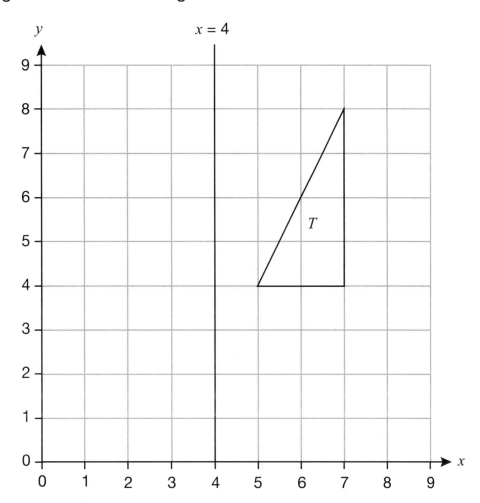

Reflect T in the line $x = 4$
Draw your answer on the grid.

[1]

7 Match each multiplier to the correct percentage change.

1.1	10% increase
0.1	90% increase
0.9	90% decrease
1.9	10% decrease

[1]

8 The grid shows two rectangles.

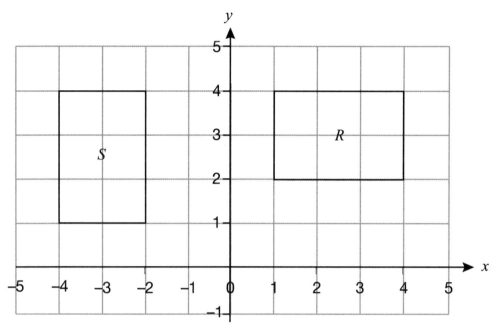

Sanjay gives this description of the transformation from rectangle R to rectangle S.

It is a rotation, centre (0, 0) by 90°.

Explain what Sanjay has missed out of his description.

_____

_____

[1]

9 Find the nth term rule for each of these sequences.

Sequence	nth term rule
1, 11, 21, 31, ...	
10, 9, 8, 7, ...	

[2]

10 The tables show information about the length and the mass of five male and five female beetles.

Male

Length (cm)	5.6	4.6	6.8	3.7	7.2
Mass (g)	5.4	4.0	5.7	3.1	6.3

Female

Length (cm)	3.2	3.8	5.4	3.6	4.5
Mass (g)	1.9	2.6	4.1	2.7	3.4

Show this information on a scatter graph.
Use the following key for your points.

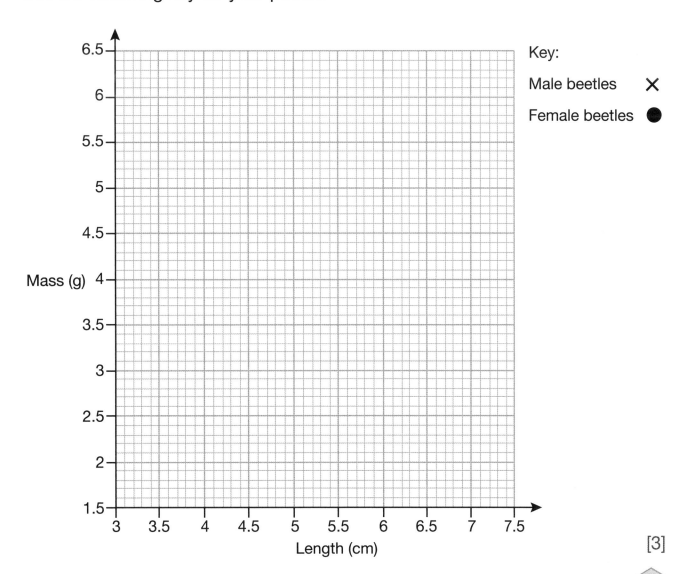

Key:

Male beetles ✕

Female beetles ●

[3]

11 A pentagon P is drawn on the grid.

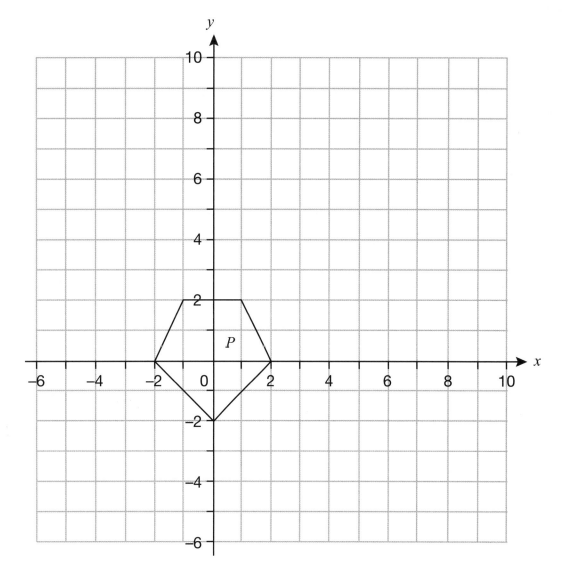

Enlarge P with scale factor 3, centre (–1, –1).

[2]

Part 2: Calculators allowed

You may use a calculator for this part of the Assessment Task.

12 Point A is mapped to point B by a reflection.

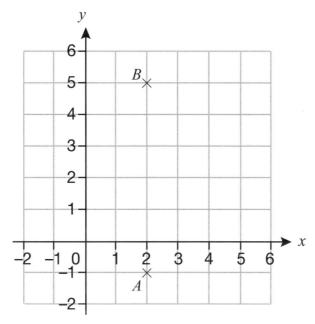

Draw a ring around the equation of the mirror line.

$x = 3$ $\qquad$ $x = 2$ $\qquad$ $y = 3$ $\qquad$ $y = 2$

[1]

13 The term-to-term rule for a sequence is: "multiply by 3 and add 6"
The second term is 18

Draw a ring around the first term.

0 $\qquad$ 4 $\qquad$ 8 $\qquad$ 60

[1]

14 The number of visitors to a museum on Monday is 700
The number of visitors to the museum on Tuesday is 35% less than on Monday.

Draw a ring around the number of visitors to the museum on Tuesday.

20 $\qquad$ 245 $\qquad$ 455 $\qquad$ 945

[1]

15 The graph shows some information about the number of sun hats a shop sold in different years.

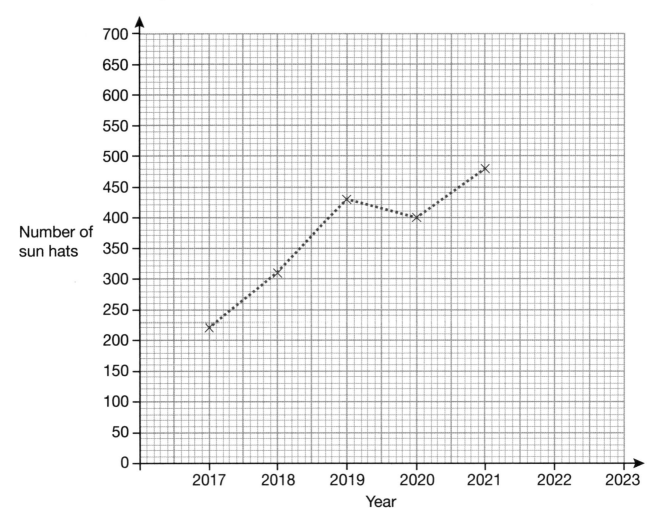

(a) The table shows the number of sun hats the shop sold in 2022 and 2023.

Year	2022	2023
Number of sun hats	520	660

Use this information to complete the graph.

[1]

(b) Describe the trend in the number of sun hats sold between 2017 and 2023.

_____

_____

[1]

16 A shape P is mapped to a shape Q by a translation.
Write each of these characteristics in the correct column of the table.
One has been done for you.

A
Number of sides

B
Size of the shape

C
Position on the grid

D
Angles of the shape

Same for shape P and shape Q	Different for shape P and shape Q
A	

[1]

17 Lauren makes a sequence of shapes from square counters.

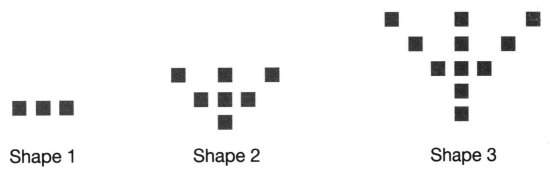

Shape 1   Shape 2   Shape 3

Shape m in Lauren's sequence contains 31 counters.

Find the value of m.

$m =$ _____

[2]

18 Triangle T is mapped to triangle U by a rotation.

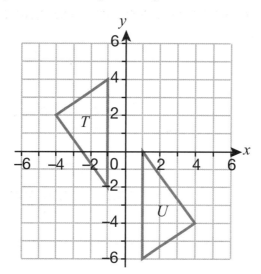

Complete the description of the rotation.

Rotation by ――――°, centre (―――――― , ――――――)

[2]

19 Two shops each sell a washing machine.

Shop 1
$450

Shop 2
$390

Shop 1 reduces their price by 12% and Shop 2 increases their price by 2.5%.

Tick (✓) the shop that now sells the washing machine at a cheaper price.

Shop 1 ☐   Shop 2 ☐

Show how you worked out your answer.

[2]

20 In 2022, a school had 60 teachers.

The pie chart shows the hair colour of the teachers at the school in 2022.

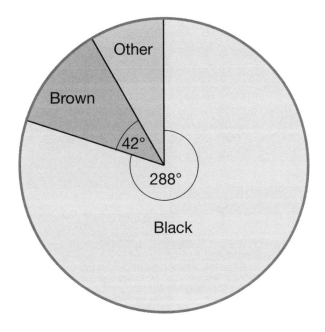

In 2023, the school has:

● 65 teachers

● the same **number** of teachers with black hair as in 2022.

Isabella draws a pie chart to show the hair colour of the teachers in 2023.

Calculate the angle for the sector representing black hair in Isabella's pie chart.

_____°

[3]

Total marks: $\dfrac{}{30}$

Assessment Task 5: Self-assessment

Enter the mark for each question in the unshaded cells below.

Question	Presenting and interpreting data 2	Transformations	Percentages	Sequences
1				
2				
3				
4				
5				
6				
7				
8				
9				
10				
11				
12				
13				
14				
15				
16				
17				
18				
19				
20				
Total	/9	/9	/5	/7

Some of the questions test your skills at Thinking and Working Mathematically. Write your marks for these questions in the grid below.

Question number	4	7	8	16	17	19	Total
Thinking and working mathematically							/8

The areas of the test that I am pleased with are

_____

_____

_____

The areas of the test that I found harder are

_____

_____

_____

Set yourself TWO targets.

TARGET 1

_____

_____

TARGET 2

_____

_____

Assessment Task 6

Answer **all** questions.
Total mark for this Assessment Task is 40.
You will need mathematical instruments.

> Topics tested:
> Chapter 21: Probability 2
> Chapter 22: Ratio and proportion
> Chapter 23: Relationships and graphs
> Chapter 24: Thinking statistically
> Chapter 25: Accurate drawing

Part 1: Calculators not allowed

Do not use a calculator for this part of the Assessment Task.

1   An empty box has mass 50 grams.
A notebook has mass 20 grams.
Sam puts x notebooks into a box.

Draw a ring around the equation that gives the total mass (y grams) of the box
and notebooks.

$$y = 20x + 50 \qquad y = x + 70 \qquad y = 50x + 20 \qquad y = 70x$$

[1]

2   Parvati and Owen share some badges in the ratio 2 : 9

Draw a circle around the fraction of the badges that Parvati gets.

$$\frac{2}{9} \qquad\qquad \frac{2}{11} \qquad\qquad \frac{9}{11} \qquad\qquad \frac{7}{9}$$

[1]

3   The table shows the number of items customers bought at a supermarket.

Number of items	Number of customers
1–10	17
11–20	22
21–30	16
31–40	11

Draw a ring around the modal class.

$$1\text{–}10 \qquad\qquad 11\text{–}20 \qquad\qquad 21\text{–}30 \qquad\qquad 31\text{–}40$$

[1]

4 The diagram shows a cuboid.

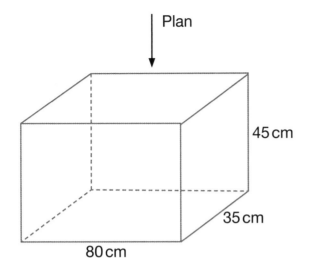

Plan

Not to scale

45 cm

35 cm

80 cm

Draw the plan view of the cuboid on the grid.
Use a scale of 1 : 10

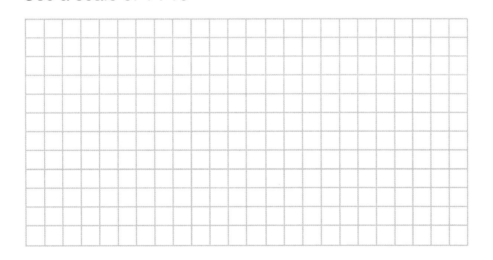

[1]

5 A man is 1.8 m tall.
A child is 80 cm tall.

Write the ratio of the height of the man to the height of the child in its simplest form.

_____ : _____

[2]

53

6 A group of 80 children and a group of 80 adults were asked to give their favourite type of soft drink.

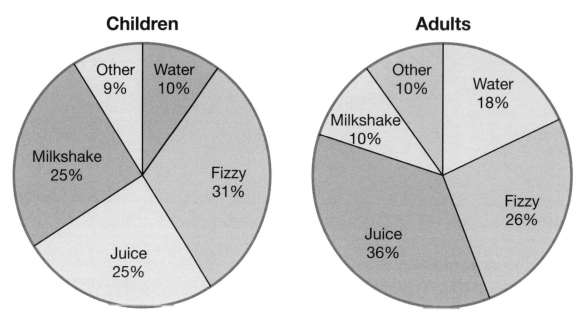

Children

Adults

(a) Compare the proportion of children who chose juice with the proportion of adults who chose juice.

_____

_____

[1]

(b) Show that 12 more children than adults said their favourite drink was a milkshake.

[1]

7 Debbie has two bags that each contain coloured balls.

Bag A contains
1 red ball
1 blue ball
1 yellow ball

Bag B contains
1 blue ball
1 green ball
1 white ball

Debbie randomly takes one ball from Bag A and one ball from Bag B.

(a) Complete the table to show all the possible combinations of colours that she can get.

Bag A	Bag B
Red	Blue
Blue	Blue

[2]

(b) Find the probability that Debbie has exactly one blue ball.

_____

[1]

8 Draw the graph of $y = 3x - 4$ for values of x between −1 and 3
You may use the table to help you.

x	−1	0	1	2	3
y					

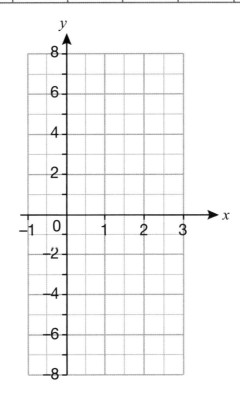

[3]

9 Draw the perpendicular bisector of the line segment AB.
You should show your construction arcs.

[2]

10 Tick (✓) to show if each point lies on the line or does not lie on the line.

Point	Lies on $y = 10 - 2x$	Does not lie on $y = 10 - 2x$
(0, 10)	☐	☐
(10, 0)	☐	☐
(4, –2)	☐	☐
(–2, 14)	☐	☐

[1]

11 Amy and Tomas share $400
Tomas receives 45% of the money.
Tomas spends all his money buying one coat, one shirt and some shoes in the following ratio.

    coat : shirt : shoes
      4 : 2 :   3

Calculate how much he spends on the shirt.

$ _____

[3]

Part 2: Calculators allowed

You may use a calculator for this part of the Assessment Task.

12 Draw a ring around the equation of the line which has a negative gradient.

$$y = 3x - 2 \qquad\qquad y = 3x + 2 \qquad\qquad y = 2x + 3 \qquad\qquad y = -2x + 3$$

[1]

13 Aishah and Megan take part in a cycling race.
The distance–time graph represents their journeys.

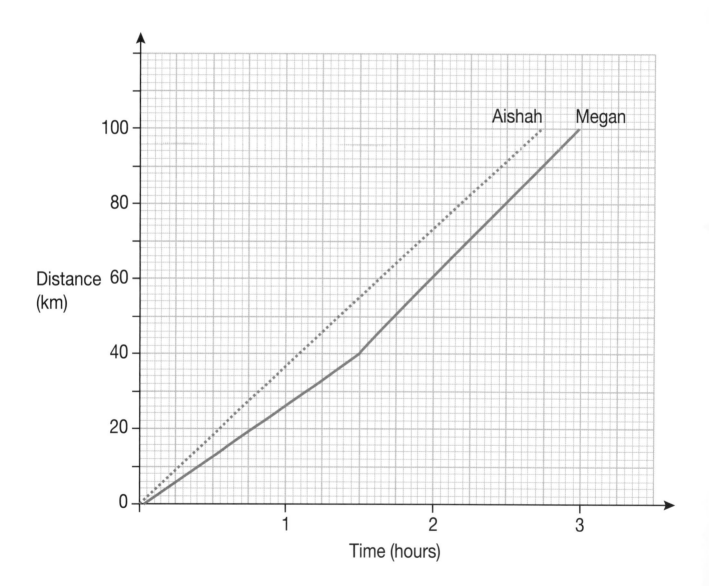

Draw a ring around the distance between Aishah and Megan after $1\frac{1}{2}$ hours.

$$10 \text{ km} \qquad\qquad 15 \text{ km} \qquad\qquad 30 \text{ km} \qquad\qquad 40 \text{ km}$$

[1]

14 The diagram shows four bags, each containing only red, yellow and green counters.
The ratio red : yellow : green counters is given for each bag.

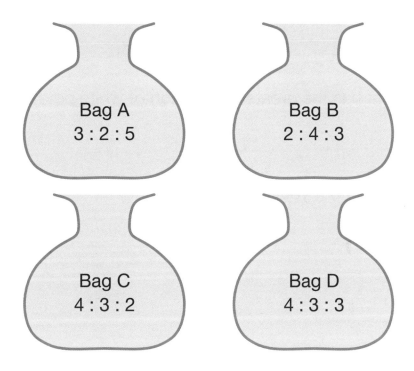

Bag A
3 : 2 : 5

Bag B
2 : 4 : 3

Bag C
4 : 3 : 2

Bag D
4 : 3 : 3

Draw a ring around the bag in which $\frac{3}{10}$ of the counters are green.

[1]

15 Use mathematical instruments to construct a triangle with sides of length 7 cm, 5 cm and 4 cm.
One side has been drawn for you.
Do not rub out your construction arcs.

7 cm

[2]

16 A farm shop sells red potatoes and white potatoes in two sizes of box.

Medium box
red : white
2 : 5

Large box
red : white
7 : 16

Tick (✓) the box that has the greater proportion of white potatoes.

Medium box   Large box ☐

Show how you worked out your answer.

[2]

17 Write down the equations of two straight lines that are parallel to $y = 6x - 7$

$y = $ _____ and $y = $ _____

[1]

18 Pierre has two fair spinners.

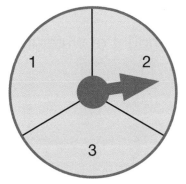 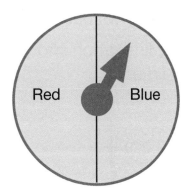

He spins each spinner once.

(a) Complete the tree diagram to show all the possible outcomes from the spins.

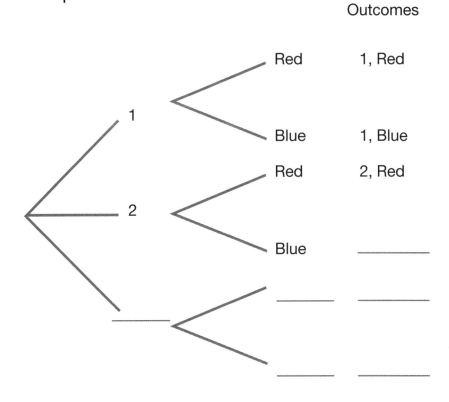

[2]

(b) Find the probability of getting an odd number on the first spinner and red on the second spinner.

_____

[1]

19 A tank contains 200 litres of water.

10 litres of water flows out of the tank every minute.

Draw a straight line graph showing how the amount of water in the tank changes with time.

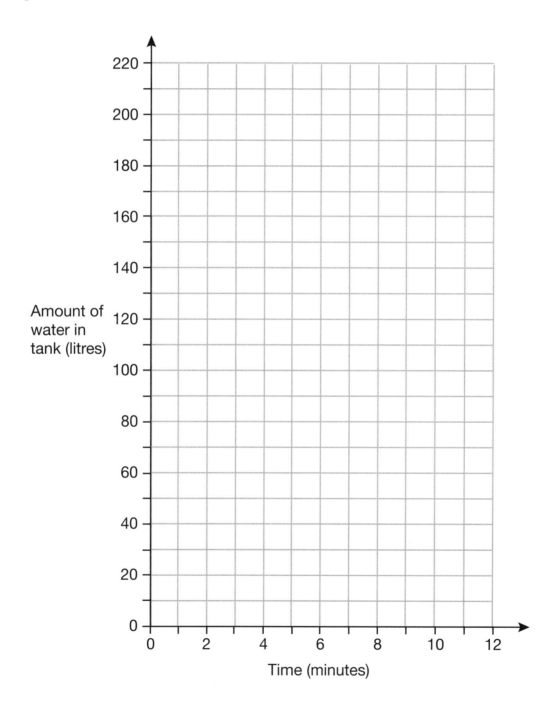

[2]

20 The stem-and-leaf diagram shows the number of apples picked from each of 15 trees in an orchard this year.

$$
\begin{array}{c|cccccc}
2 & 3 & 4 & 4 & 5 & 8 & 8 \\
3 & 1 & 2 & 5 & 9 & 9 \\
4 & 0 & 3 & 7 \\
5 & 2
\end{array}
$$

Key   2 | 3   represents 23 apples

(a) Complete the table to show the median and range of the number of apples.

median	
range	

[2]

(b) The median and range of the number of apples picked from the same trees **last year** were

median = 38   and   range = 19

Compare the number of apples picked this year with the number picked last year.

_____

_____

_____

_____

[2]

21 Walter and Eva play a game involving throwing two six-sided dice.

Dice 1	Dice 2
Numbered 1, 2, 2, 3, 5, 6	Numbered 1, 1, 1, 4, 5, 6

They throw each dice once and add together the numbers to get a total score.

Walter wins if the total score is **less than** 7
Otherwise, Eva wins.

Show that Walter has a higher chance of winning than Eva.
You may use the sample space diagram to help you.

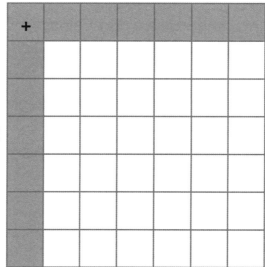

Dice 1

Dice 2

[3]

Total marks: ——
40

Assessment Task 6: Self-assessment

Enter the mark for each question in the unshaded cells below.

Question	Probability 2	Ratio and proportion	Relationships and graphs	Thinking statistically	Accurate drawing
1					
2					
3					
4					
5					
6					
7					
8					
9					
10					
11					
12					
13					
14					
15					
16					
17					
18					
19					
20					
21					
Total	/9	/9	/10	/7	/5

Some of the questions test your skills at Thinking and Working Mathematically. Write your marks for these questions in the grid below.

Question number	6(b)	10	17	21	Total
Thinking and working mathematically					/6

The areas of the test that I am pleased with are

_____

_____

_____

The areas of the test that I found harder are

_____

_____

_____

Set yourself TWO targets.

TARGET 1

_____

_____

TARGET 2

_____

_____

End of Book Test: Paper 1

Answer **all** questions.
Total marks for this paper: 50
You will need mathematical instruments for this test.
You may find tracing paper useful.

Calculators not allowed

1 Draw a ring around the value of (–2) × (–6)

    –12   –8   8   12

[1]

2 Calculate the value of $\frac{4y-3}{3}$ when $y = 6$

    4   5   7   9

[1]

3 Calculate $6 \div \frac{1}{3}$

    18   2 $\frac{1}{2}$ $\frac{1}{18}$

[1]

4 Calculate the volume of the triangular prism.

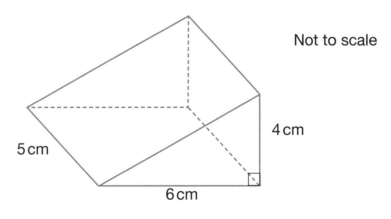

Not to scale

4 cm

5 cm

6 cm

    15 cm³   30 cm³   60 cm³   120 cm³

[1]

5 Erika throws a biased dice.
The table shows the probability of each outcome.

Score on dice	1	2	3	4	5	6
Probability	$\dfrac{1}{16}$	$\dfrac{1}{16}$	$\dfrac{3}{16}$	$\dfrac{5}{16}$	$\dfrac{3}{16}$	$\dfrac{3}{16}$

Find the probability that Erika's score is **not** 4

$\dfrac{1}{6}$ $\qquad\qquad$ $\dfrac{5}{6}$ $\qquad\qquad$ $\dfrac{5}{16}$ $\qquad\qquad$ $\dfrac{11}{16}$

[1]

6 The table shows the mass of some letters.

Mass, m (grams)	Frequency
$0 \leqslant m < 50$	7
$50 \leqslant m < 100$	9
$100 \leqslant m < 150$	6
$150 \leqslant m < 200$	2

Draw a ring around the number of letters with a mass of less than 150 grams.

6 $\qquad\qquad$ 15 $\qquad\qquad$ 16 $\qquad\qquad$ 22

[1]

7 A sequence has first term 3
The term-to-term rule is multiply by 3 and subtract 4

Write each number in the correct column of the table to show if it is a term in the sequence or not.

3 $\qquad\qquad$ 5 $\qquad\qquad$ 7 $\qquad\qquad$ 9 $\qquad\qquad$ 11

The first number has been written in for you.

A term in the sequence	Not a term in the sequence.
3	

[1]

8 Write down the square roots of 49

_____ and _____

[1]

9 **(a)** x is an integer.
x satisfies the inequality $0 \leqslant x < 4$

List all the possible values of x.

_____

[1]

(b) y is a number that is greater than 2 and less than 6

Write the possible values of y as an inequality.

_____ y _____

[1]

10 Calculate

$40 \times 0.65 \times 0.25$

_____

[2]

11 Translate triangle T by vector $\begin{pmatrix} 2 \\ -3 \end{pmatrix}$.

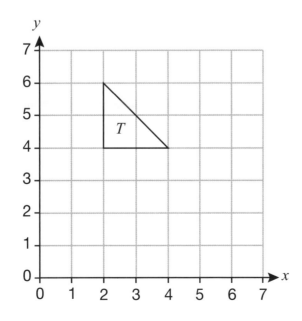

[1]

12 Match each diagram to the type of angles it shows.

Diagram	Type of angle

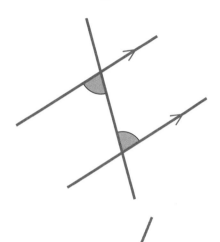

Vertically opposite

Corresponding angles

Alternate angles

[1]

13 Calculate.

-5×0.3 _____

1.2×0.6 _____

[2]

14 The compound bar chart shows some information about the types of vehicles passing a house on different days.

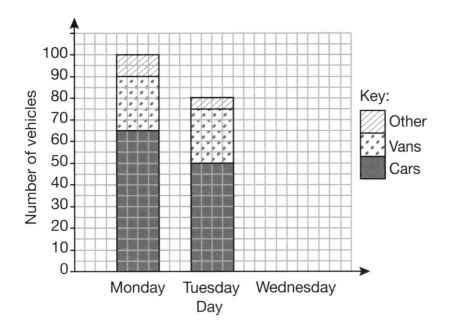

(a) Find how many more cars passed the house on Monday than on Tuesday.

_____

[2]

(b) On Wednesday, the following vehicles passed the house.

    60 cars,   20 vans and   15 other vehicles

Complete the compound bar chart by showing this information.

[2]

15 Amol says,

    *'If a quadrilateral has perpendicular diagonals **and** does not have 4 right angles then it must be a rhombus.'*

Explain why Amol is wrong.

_____

_____

[1]

16 Toby has answered each of these questions about powers incorrectly.
Write the correct answer in the final column.

	Toby's answer	Correct answer
Simplify 11^0	11	
Simplify $11^5 \times 11$	121^5	
Simplify $11^{10} \div 11^2$	11^5	

[2]

17 (a) Expand the brackets.

$2x(3x - 5)$

_____

[1]

(b) Factorise.

$12h^2 + 30h$

_____

[2]

18 Here are two calculation questions.
A student has attempted each question.

Put a tick (✓) or a cross (✗) next to each answer to show if the work
is correct or not.

Question 1: $\sqrt{16 + 4 \times 5}$

Answer: $\sqrt{16} = 4$
$4 \times 5 = 20$
So, $\sqrt{16 + 4 \times 5} = 4 + 20 = 24$ _____

Question 2: $\dfrac{4^3}{8 - 2 \times 2}$

Answer: $4^3 = 64$
$8 - 2 \times 2 = 8 - 4 = 4$
So, $\dfrac{4^3}{8 - 2 \times 2} = \dfrac{64}{4} = 16$ _____

[1]

19 Construct triangle ABC with $AB = 6.2$ cm, angle $CAB = 105°$ and $BC = 8.5$ cm.
Do not rub out your construction arcs.
The point A has been marked for you.

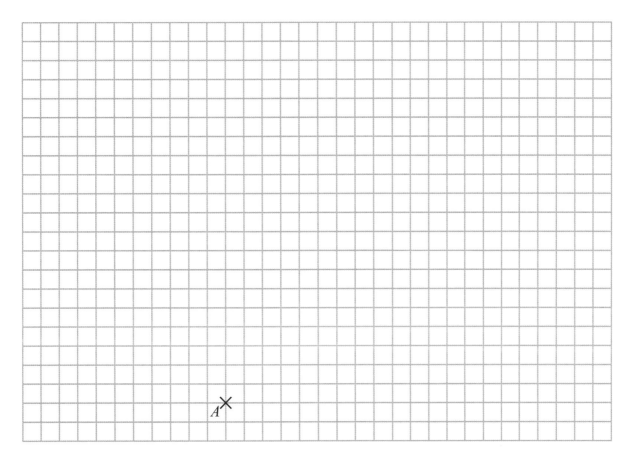

[2]

20 Find the coordinates of the midpoint of the line segment joining (–13, –8)
to (–1, 14).

(———— , ————)

[2]

21 Here is a function machine.

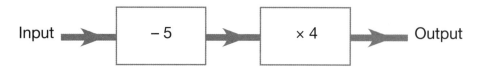

Input → − 5 → × 4 → Output

Complete the input–output table for this function.

Input	Output
−3	
	20
	2

[2]

22 Work out $4\frac{2}{5} - 1\frac{3}{4}$

Give your answer as a mixed number in its simplest form.

[3]

23 Rita paints white plates.
She paints the edge of each plate either yellow
or green or red.
She paints a spot on each plate that is either red
or blue or black.

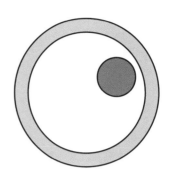

(a) Complete the tree diagram to show all the possible
combinations of colours.

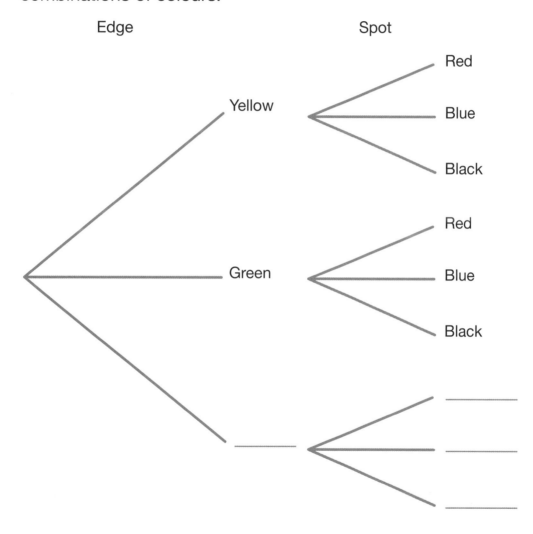

[1]

(b) Rita chooses one of the combinations of colours at random to
paint a plate.

Find the probability that the plate has some red on it.

.... [1]

24 The grid shows a quadrilateral P.

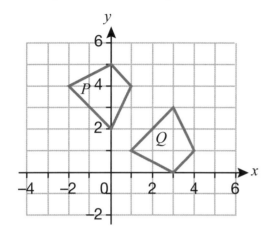

P is rotated to give quadrilateral Q.

Complete the description of the rotation from P to Q.

A rotation of _____° in a _____ direction,

centre point (0, _____).

[2]

25 A cyclist is cycling 160 **km** over three days.

On day 1, the cyclist travels 32 **miles**.
On day 2, the cyclist travels 38 miles.

Work out how far, in kilometres, the cyclist has left to travel on day 3.

_____km

[2]

26 Here is part of a multiplication grid.

×	0.1	0.01
77		
		0.0054

Find the four missing numbers and write them in the table.

[2]

27 Solve.

$$4(3 - 2x) = 39 - 3(x + 4)$$

$x =$ _____

[3]

28 The diagram shows a trapezium $ACDF$.

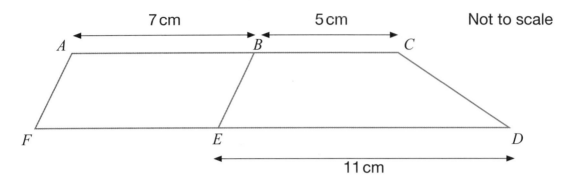

B is a point on the line AC and E is a point on the line FD.
AF is parallel to BE.

The area of $ABEF$ is 42 cm².

Show that the area of the trapezium $ACDF$ is 90 cm².

[3]

Total marks: $\dfrac{}{50}$

End of Book Test: Paper 2

Answer **all** questions.
Total marks for this paper: 50
You will need mathematical instruments for this test.

Calculators allowed

1 Draw a ring around the fraction that is greater than 0.7

$$\frac{2}{3} \qquad\qquad \frac{17}{25} \qquad\qquad \frac{11}{16} \qquad\qquad \frac{5}{7}$$

[1]

2 Anita has n bricks.
Paddy has half as many bricks as Anita.

Draw a ring around the number of bricks that Paddy has.

$$n + \frac{1}{2} \qquad\qquad n - \frac{1}{2} \qquad\qquad \frac{1}{2}\,n \qquad\qquad 2n$$

[1]

3 The diagram shows the position of a school (S), a tower (T) and a farm (F).

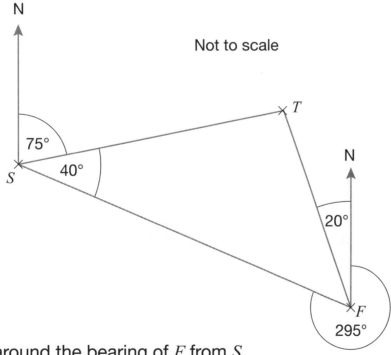

Draw a ring around the bearing of F from S.

$$295° \qquad\qquad 115° \qquad\qquad 040° \qquad\qquad 020°$$

[1]

4 A graph has equation $y = 2x + 1$

Draw a ring around the coordinates of the point that lies on the graph.

(0, 1)   (1, 2)   (2, 2)   (3, 2)

[1]

5 The order of rotation symmetry for a regular polygon is 24

Draw a ring around the number of its sides.

6   12   24   48

[1]

6 The scatter graph shows the length and width of five paintings drawn by each of two artists.

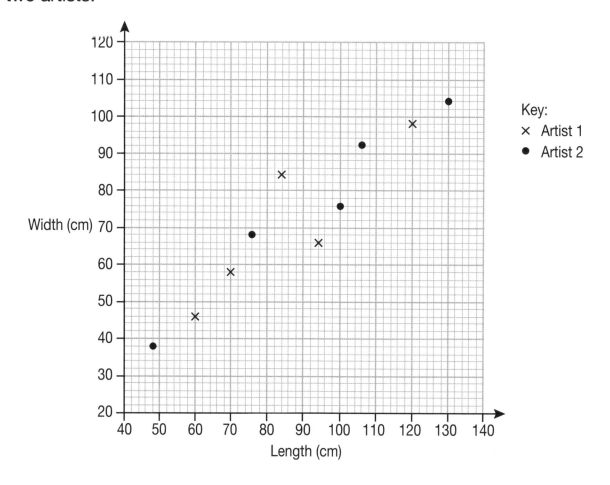

Key:
× Artist 1
● Artist 2

Draw a ring around the smallest length of the paintings painted by Artist 1.

38 cm   46 cm   48 cm   60 cm

[1]

7 Tick (✓) to show if each statement is true or false.

	True	False
−125 is a negative cube number	☐	☐
The cube root of 1000 is 10	☐	☐
$\sqrt[3]{-64} = -8$	☐	☐

[1]

8 The grid shows a triangle C and a triangle E.

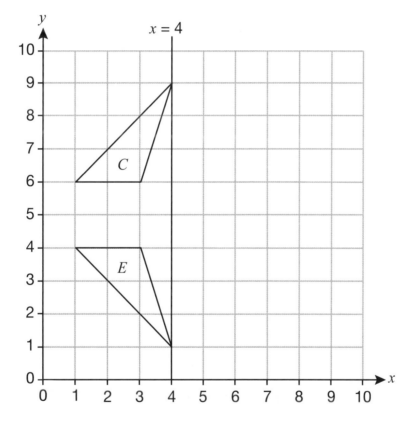

(a) Reflect triangle C in the line $x = 4$.

Label your image D.

[1]

(b) Triangle E is a reflection of triangle C.

Write down the equation of the mirror line for this reflection.

_____

[1]

9 Hamza has some cards.

Card A	Card B	Card C	Card D
$y = 2x - 3$	$5x$	$6a - 2b + c$	$3n - 2 = 31$

Each card contains an expression, an equation or a formula.

Write each card in the correct column of the table.
One has been done for you.

Expression	Equation	Formula
		Card A

[1]

10 Alfie and Sofia find some stamps.
They share the stamps in the ratio 5 : 7

(a) Write down the fraction of the stamps that Alfie receives.

_____

[1]

(b) Write down a possible value for the total number of stamps that Alfie and Sofia find.

_____

[1]

11 Round each number to 1 significant figure.

(a) 494 _____

[1]

(b) 0.00447 _____

[1]

12 Nihal has a bag that contains four counters numbered 1, 2, 3 and 4
He takes one counter from the bag.
He puts it back into the bag and then takes a second counter.

(a) Complete the sample space diagram showing the possible numbers on the two counters Nihal takes.

2nd counter

		1	2	3	4
1st counter	1	1, 1	1, 2	1, 3	
	2	2, 1	2, 2	2, 3	
	3	3, 1	3, 2	3, 3	
	4	4, 1	4, 2	4, 3	

[1]

(b) Find the probability that the two counters both have a number greater than 3

_____

[1]

13 Find the size of the angle x.

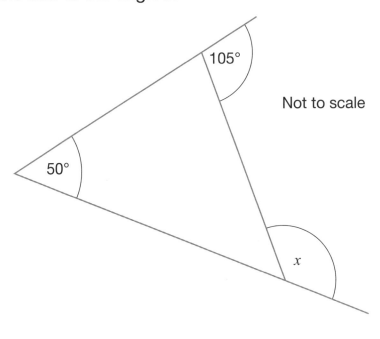

105°

Not to scale

50°

x

$x =$ _____ °

[2]

14 (a) The stem-and-leaf diagram shows the ages of the first 10 customers at a café on Monday.

```
2 | 6
3 | 2  4  7
4 | 1  7  8
5 | 2  3
6 | 6
```

Key: 2 | 6 represents 26 years

The next two customers at the café on Monday were 55 and 39 years old.

Add the ages of these two customers to the stem-and-leaf diagram.

[1]

(b) The median ages of all the customers at the café on Tuesday and Wednesday are shown below.

Median on Tuesday	Median on Wednesday
47	55

Complete this comparison of the ages of the customers on these two days.

Customers are on average older on _____

Write Tuesday or Wednesday here.

because the median for this day was _____

Write smaller or larger here.

[1]

15 In this question all lengths are in centimetres.
The diagram shows a trapezium *ABCD*.

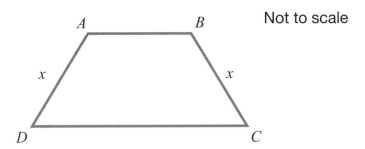

$AD = BC = x$

AB is 1 cm longer than *AD*.
DC is twice the length of *AB*.

Find an expression for the perimeter of *ABCD*.
Give your answer in terms of x and in its simplest form.

_____

[2]

16 Maria is investigating how students in her school feel about waste plastic.
She wants to choose a sample of 50 students from her school.
She thinks about asking the first 50 students who arrive at school one day.

(a) Write down one advantage of Maria's sampling method.

_____

_____

[1]

(b) Describe a better way that Maria could collect a sample of 50 students.

_____

_____

[1]

17 A company uses the following rule to find the cost for hiring a van.

There is a fixed cost of $40

and

an additional charge of $50 per day hired.

Use the grid to draw a graph showing the cost of hiring the van (C) plotted against the number of days hired (n).

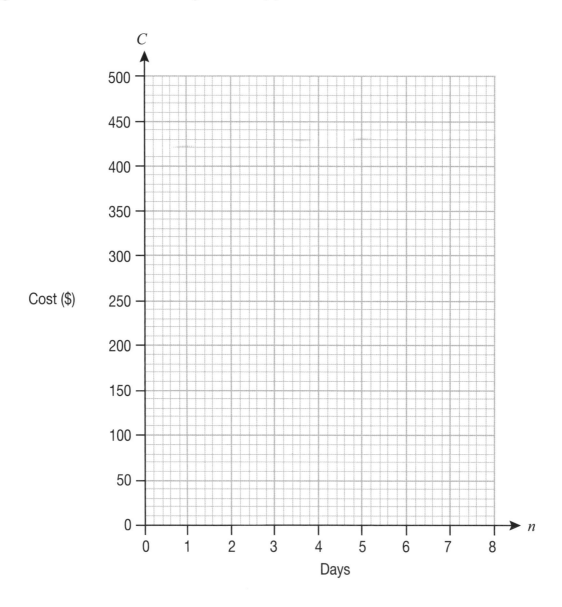

[2]

18 The grid shows a shape P and a shape Q.

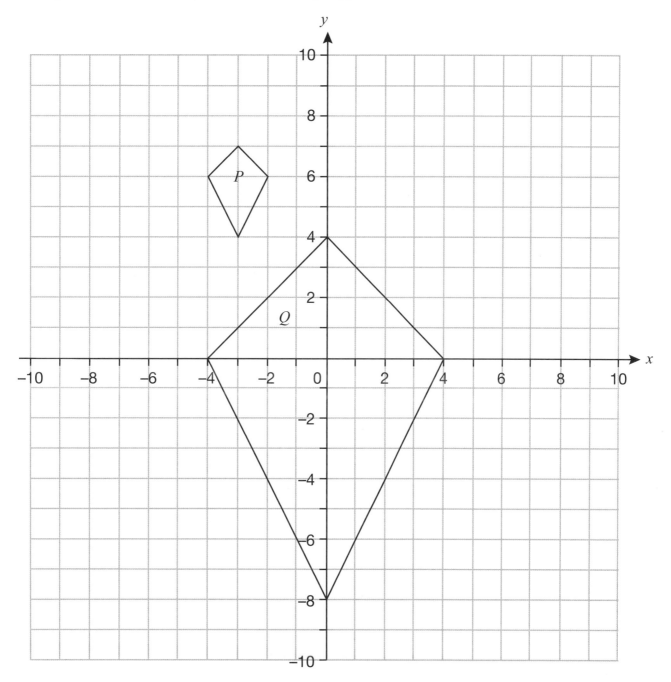

(a) Write down the scale factor of the enlargement from P to Q.

_____

[1]

(b) Enlarge shape P by scale factor 2, centre $(-9, 5)$.

[2]

19 The table shows information about the mass (in grams) of 90 birds.

Mass, m (grams)	Frequency
$14 \leqslant m < 16$	9
$16 \leqslant m < 18$	15
$18 \leqslant m < 20$	39
$20 \leqslant m < 22$	21
$22 \leqslant m < 24$	6

Draw a frequency diagram to show this information.

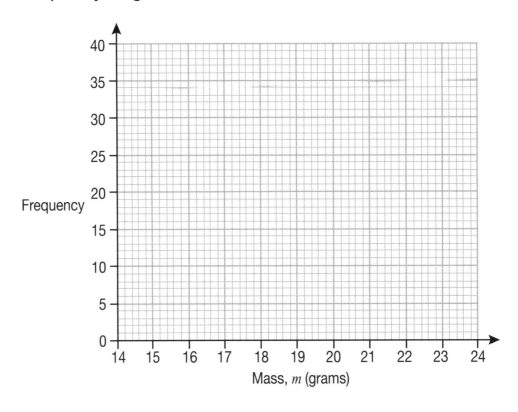

[2]

20 Make p the subject of this formula.

$$R = \frac{p + 5}{3}$$

[2]

21 The prime factorisation of 300 is $2^2 \times 3 \times 5^2$

The prime factorisation of 440 is $2^3 \times 5 \times p$ where p is a prime number.

Find the lowest common multiple of 300 and 440

_____

[2]

22 A box contains 112 pens.
The pens are blue, red or black in the following ratio:

blue : red : black = 7 : 2 : 5

10 of the **black** pens do not work.

Find the percentage of black pens that do not work.

_____ %

[3]

23 The diagram shows a prism made from joining together two cuboids.

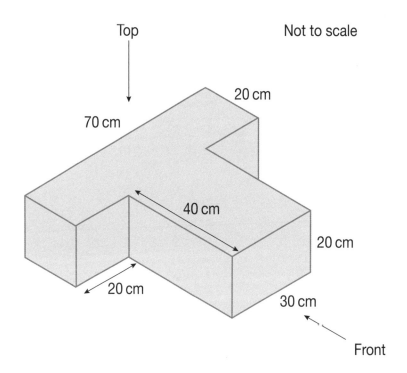

Top

Not to scale

70 cm

20 cm

40 cm

20 cm

20 cm

30 cm

Front

A scale drawing of the plan view of the prism is shown below.

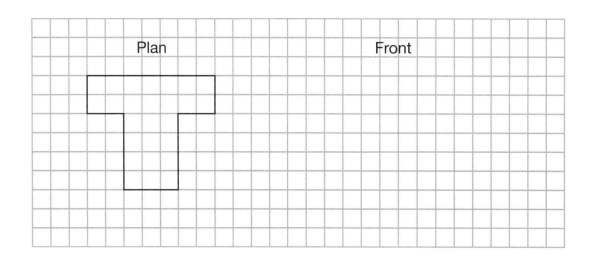

Plan

Front

Draw the front elevation of the prism using the same scale.

[2]

24 The distance from Town A to Town B is 120 km.
Oleksii travels from Town A to Town B.
His journey is represented on the distance–time graph.

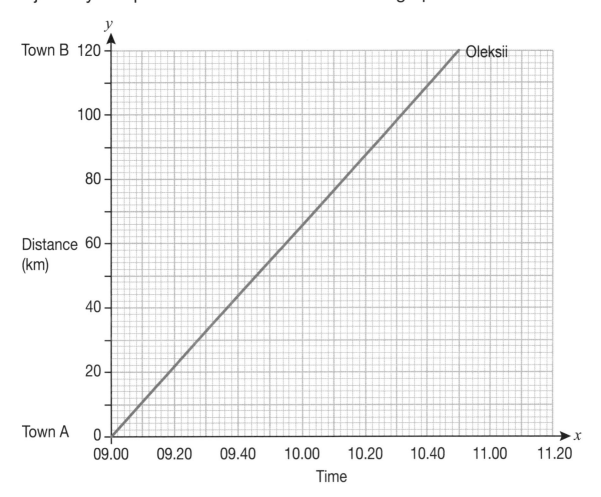

Asma travels at a constant speed from **Town B to Town A**.
She leaves Town B 10 minutes after Oleksii leaves Town A.

Asma takes 20 minutes longer to complete her journey than Oleksii takes for his journey.

Use the distance–time graph to find the time when Asma and Oleksii pass each other.

_____

[2]

25 A packet of 20 biscuits costs $1.50

The number of biscuits in a packet decreases by 10%.
The cost of a packet increases by 8%.

Show that, after both changes, each biscuit costs $0.09

[3]

26 A bicycle has a wheel of radius 28 cm.
On a journey, the wheel turns around 600 times.

Darren says the length of the journey is more than 1 kilometre.
Tick (✓) to show if he is correct or not.

Darren is correct. ☐   Darren is not correct.

Show how you worked out your answer.

[3]

27 The 2nd term of a linear sequence is 11
The 5th term of the sequence is 20

Find the 100th term of the sequence.

_____

[2]

Total marks: ——
50

End of Book Test: Self-assessment

Enter the mark for each question for Paper 1 and Paper 2 in the unshaded cells.

Paper 1

Question	Number	Algebra	Geometry and Measure	Statistics and Probability
1				
2				
3				
4				
5				
6				
7				
8				
9				
10				
11				
12				
13				
14				
15				
16				
17				
18				
19				
20				
21				
22				
23				
24				
25				
26				
27				
28				
Total P1	/15	/12	/15	/8

Paper 2

Question	Number	Algebra	Geometry and Measure	Statistics and Probability
1				
2				
3				
4				
5				
6				
7				
8				
9				
10				
11				
12				
13				
14				
15				
16				
17				
18				
19				
20				
21				
22				
23				
24				
25				
26				
27				
Total P2	/14	/13	/14	/9

Overall total Paper 1 + Paper 2:

Total	/29	/25	/29	/17

Total mark: _____ /100

95

Thinking and working mathematically

Some of the questions test your skills at Thinking and Working Mathematically.
Write your marks for these questions in the grids below.

Paper 1

Question number	7	12	15	16	18	28	Total
Thinking and working mathematically							/9

Paper 2

Question number	7	9	10(b)	16(a)	16(b)	25	27	Total
Thinking and working mathematically								/10

Overall total: _____ /19

The areas of the test that I am pleased with are

The areas of the test that I found harder are

Set yourself THREE targets.

TARGET 1

TARGET 2

TARGET 3